M000309315

FROM
TRAUMA
TO
TRIUMPH

FROM

TRAUMA

TO

TRIUMPH

DR. ANISSA M. JONES

FROM TRAUMA TO TRIUMPH
Published by Purposely Created Publishing Group™
Copyright © 2020 Anissa M. Jones
All rights reserved.

No part of this book may be reproduced, distributed or transmitted in any form by any means, graphic, electronic, or mechanical, including photocopy, recording, taping, or by any information storage or retrieval system, without permission in writing from the publisher, except in the case of reprints in the context of reviews, quotes, or references.

Printed in the United States of America
ISBN: 978-1-64484-200-3

Special discounts are available on bulk quantity purchases by book clubs, associations and special interest groups. For details email: sales@publishyourgift.com or call (888) 949-6228. For information log on to www.PublishYourGift.com

I would like to dedicate this book to the memory of my grandmother, Annie Lois Pennymon, who I fondly referred to as Pennymame. She was my first business investor and my first teacher. I also dedicate this to my mother who told me that I am beautiful and how proud she was to be my mother. They both believed that I would make an impact on the world. They were absolutely on target.

[TABLE OF CONTENTS]

[FOREWORD]

I was extremely humbled and honored when Dr. Anissa Jones asked me to write the foreword of her new book, *From Trauma to Triumph: An Entrepreneur's Guide to Starting Over*. But, before I begin, a little history first. I met Anissa when she was fifteen years old at my first office in 1986. She and her grandmother came to my office for treatment of injuries following an automobile accident. I can still remember her bright eyes and beautiful smile on her first visit. She responded very well to chiropractic treatment and became interested in the profession. I remember her asking many questions and I was so proud when she chose my alma mater, Life Chiropractic College, now Life University, to pursue her degree. I still have the ambassador diploma Life University sent me recognizing my referral.

Now, after twenty-one years in practice, she has been both a leader in our profession as a Middle Georgia district Georgia Chiropractic Association President and ambassador for new practitioners, and in our city of Macon, Georgia, as an elected official with our water authority board when she was elected in 2018. Anissa is also well known as a professor in the science departments of several of our local colleges and universities. And if she wasn't busy enough, she also owns a local popular women's clothing store, The Pink Chief Boutique.

But one of the greatest things I love about Anissa is she has always given back to the community with her service to the needy and homeless with her volunteer work, serving meals over the holidays. She is considered a success by everyone who knows her and she really "talks the talk" and "walks the walk." As an old-timer who has been on the Georgia Chiropractic Association board of directors for years and immediate past president, I sometimes worry about the future and direction of my profession in the healthcare world. It is so refreshing when you see extraordinary young visionaries like Anissa ready to take your place to advance your profession. I know chiropractic will be in good hands when I'm gone!

Anissa has written this powerful new book that will take the reader on her journey from tragedies in life to a very successful businesswoman. It is a powerful blueprint to self-worth, success, and freedom, as well. You will find *From Trauma to Triumph* to be not only a positive inspiration but also fun, educational, interesting, and just an overall wonderful read. I know you will enjoy it.

Thank you, Dr. Jones, for allowing me to participate in your writing endeavor. You are a great author, peer, and human being. And I'm proud to call you my friend. Good luck and God bless you and our chiropractic family.

Dr. G. Clark Stull

[INTRODUCTION]

This book will take you on a journey with me as I reveal the lessons I learned from the tragedies to become the successful businesswoman I am today. My hope is that this blueprint guides you to a path that brings you success and self-worth. Embark with me as we navigate the storms that mentally prepared me for my purpose. The ultimate stop is FREEDOM.

As a small child, I had the good fortune of growing up with my grandmother, who was also my first investor. She gave me the opportunity to create my first company in high school. It was a mobile candy store. It was birthed out of necessity. My sister and I were members of the band and wanted to go on the band trip. We didn't have much, but she gave me and my sister the seed money, and we went shopping to buy candy. By the time the year was over, we accumulated funds well over our goal. My grandmother also was a believer and practitioner of homeopathic methods and remedies. I would watch her in amazement as she would "whip up" concoctions in the kitchen that treated everything from a sore throat to a cut on your foot. My grandmother would say, "The Lord put in us all we need to survive; sometimes it just needs a little help." This sparked my interest in becoming a holistic doctor. Imagine my surprise when the very same thing my grandmother said to me was echoed to me when I started my educational journey in chiropractic school. This was a full circle moment for me. I graduated from chiropractic school at the top of my class. I was one of three black students to graduate. I was full of hope, and my grandmother was there to see it all. That was the proudest moment in my life, my grandmother witnessing me become a doctor and no longer being a "professional student" as she would call me. She thought I'd never finish school. On that day, I presented her with a PHT (putting her through) degree. You would have thought that I had given her a million dollars. She was so proud.

I opened my practice, and I was the first African American to practice in my city. I became the leading chiropractic facility in Macon, GA. I was even a Black history moment. Can I tell you something that I am not proud of? It was the unthinkable. I lost my million-dollar practice. I allowed another person to take everything from me I had worked so hard for. I can still smell the trash from the alley as I was packing up the remainder of my things that were left behind. It was a hot summer's day, and two people I hardly knew were helping me savage the remnants of my practice. I cried the entire time. All I could hear was my grandmother telling me that I deserved better and that I was better than this. So, what do you do when you've reached rock bottom? You start from scratch. I rebuilt my practice. I knew this time, I wanted to create a foolproof system and plan that would get me back to million-dollar profits in a shorter period. It has been five years since my grandmother passed, but I still receive wisdom and guidance from her daily. She was my first business teacher. I am here because my grandmother saved my life. Now, I get to save other business owners from going down the same rabbit hole I did. I get to help you successfully open your own business without making the costly mistakes. This way, your goal each day is to make sure you create a hassle-free environment where your clients can thrive, and you can concentrate solely on getting "totally fuzed" about YOU.

CHAPTER 1

STAND IN YOUR STORY

Picture if you will a little black girl from Macon, GA who was a little awkward but dared to dream and thrive. I fondly remember my mother being very driven to make sure we had what we needed. Life wasn't easy; there were trials, tests, and triumphs that all helped to mold me into the person I am today. We grew up in a faith-based home, devoted Christians. I never in a million years thought I would spiral into the life I experienced. At the age of seven, I experienced what was the first of many exposures to molestation. I was in the second grade when another male student touched me inappropriately. I told him I was going to tell the teacher what he did, but he pushed me so hard that I was too afraid to tell anyone about the incident. Prior to this incident, my personality was pretty level, a loving, mild-mannered, average child. Afterwards, I became combative, snarky, and rebellious. I didn't trust anyone. During this time, my mother was on her second marriage, and we moved a lot, and we were in church a lot. Fast forward a few more years. My mother was married to her third husband. The first few months were good and stable. We moved to a wonderful neighborhood, and life was starting to normalize. One night I was asleep in a room that I shared with my sister, and I felt a shadow over me. I thought I was dreaming, but I was not. My stepfather was standing over me. He made me get out of the bed to "fondle him." This was the start of nightly visits from him. The touching rapidly escalated to him performing sexual acts with me. He threatened to kill my mother if I ever said anything. Not only was I being sexual abused, but he was also physically abusing my mother. I believed him. I was living in my own prison within myself. I needed an escape!. But what?

I always excelled in school. Even with all the things happening around me, I used school to escape the turmoil. Books took me to a place I could have never imagined. Through books, I could be anything, from a princess in a castle in England to a hunter on an African safari. Books made me want more. They challenged my everyday existence. I wanted more for myself. I figured out at an early age I wanted to experience everything I had read about. I remember our family owning a set of World Book encyclopedias. My sister and I always envisioned ourselves in the encyclopedia. The use of encyclopedias is outdated now, but Google is the same concept. I continued to work hard in school even though we didn't have much monetarily speaking.

By the time I was out of middle school, we moved in with my grandmother. She provided strength, guidance, and stability when I needed it most. We ended up with her because at this time, my mother had divorced her husband and spiraled into a cycle of misfortunes. (That's another story for my mother to tell.) My grandmother taught me so much about faith and hard work. During this time, I focused on my education even more. I could see what the future looked like for me.

I quickly moved up the education ladder in high school and obtained a 3.75 GPA. I found a love for science. I knew then I wanted to be a doctor. Initially, I thought I wanted to go to medical school and become an Ob/Gyn. I asked my grandmother to take me to the library, so I could get as many books to read on what the steps were to become a doctor. Unfortunately, I didn't have any guidance from counselors at school about where and how to start the process of going to college. I was self-taught. We went to the library and spent hours getting all the resources we needed. At the time, my grandmother had not received her business degree, but she was wise and understood the power of a good education.

During my senior year in high school, I overheard other students talking about college and being in college preparatory programs outside of the classes we all were attending at school. They were sharing stories about the SAT and the ACT tests that were coming up. I was in awe. I immediately asked my grandmother to take me to the library, so I could get a book on what to do to take these tests. With the assistance of my grandmother, I sent off the application and fees. I, then, set out to apply for college. I was on my way or so I thought.

I was accepted into many schools including UGA, Spelman, FAMU, and Howard. I decided to go to Savannah State because it was the most economical choice. I followed the money. I was given a full academic scholarship. This was the first time I would not have my grandmother to help me stay on track. College was exciting and frightening all in one. I made new friends and settled into my new life away from home. I had no experiences with the opposite sex that were healthy or rewarding, so I was always skeptical. I always traveled in large groups. On one uneventful day, the group decided to attend an off-campus party. I remember feeling very vulnerable and afraid to go. That was my opportunity to say no, but peer pressure is a force that sometimes can't be denied. Later that evening, I noticed that some of the people I came with were not there. I ran outside to see if the car was still there. To my surprise, no car. I panicked. I then proceeded to look for some of the others. I didn't see anyone. I searched the building where the party was held, and then the incident I will never forget took place. I was raped by a group of male students. How many?, I do not know because I was blindfolded, gagged, and bound. Here was another incident of me being violated. Why was my essence as a woman being hijacked? Why was my essence being tested? After they were done, I found myself in an abandoned building unable to move. I lay there for what felt like days. Eventually, a man found me in a closet. I later found out that it was out of this person's routine to even check on this building on that day. He grabbed a blanket from his truck, put it around me, and then helped me get free. My initial reaction was to kick and scream. He was a stranger as well. He located my clothes and proceeded to ask me where I lived. He asked me what happened and immediately took me to the campus police office. This time I was not going to be afraid. I explained to campus police what happened to me. They got a female officer to take me to the hospital where a doctor examined me using a rape kit. Unfortunately, since I was blindfolded, I could not identify my assailants, and the officers had nothing to go on but the few details I could provide. The positive thing that happened was it changed a few policies to make sure other female students were safe on campus.

The next days on campus were filled with rumors and facial expressions that made the lady from the *Scarlet Letter* look like a nun. I quickly became the brunt of all the jokes and commentary. I took the walk of shame every day. It made college life unbearable, and to make matters worse, I became pregnant as a result of the rape. I had to call my grandmother to tell her that I was pregnant. I was too ashamed to tell her what happened, and I never did. Now, you are probably thinking to yourself, "I thought this was a guide about starting over in business." And it is. You need to know a few personal things about me to fully understand my process and see how I operate. Remember the title is *From Trauma to Triumph.*

Due to the pregnancy, I found myself in a really dark place. I was full of guilt. At the age of 19, I had the epic task of deciding whether to keep the child or to have an abortion.. Simply put, I kept the child. Coming from a devout Christian family, abortion was not an option. Neither my grandmother nor my mother was excited about the pregnancy. I felt like the ugly stepchild, and in my mind, my mother was embarrassed to say the least. Remember, I never told them about the rape incident. Most of my experiences up to this point would probably have most people in a sea of depression with lost hope but not me. I had dreams, aspirations, ambitions, and drive. I wasn't going to be a statistic. I was going to make something out of myself. I was going to do it.

I finished my sophomore year at Savannah State remotely. They called it correspondence courses. I did schoolwork by mail and went to campus to take mid-terms and final exams. During this time, my mom had gotten her life back on track, and my sister and brother were living in the house with her. I decided to live with my grandmother who cared for me throughout the entire pregnancy. One night I was taking a shower, and I noticed a gelatinous glob on the bottom of the tub. I was terrified. I ran to get my grandmother, so she could tell me what it was. My grandmother had a sense of humor. She simply said, "We bout to have a baby." Evidently my water had broken, and I didn't know it. It's 1991, and my grandmother and grandfather had just purchased their brand-new Oldsmobile. It was blue and had a beautiful interior with the wood grain finishes. It was fully loaded and had all the bells and whistles. I swiftly got dressed to go to the hospital and had my bags ready to go. My grandmother, on the other hand, had a different plan. She was meticulously placing plastic all over the car. In her mind, I was not about to mess up her new car having a baby. So, after ten minutes of prep time, we are finally on the road to the hospital. Mind you- I was a military brat, so we had to go to the base hospital about thirty-five minutes away.

We arrived at the hospital, and I was placed in a birthing room, and contractions are rapidly close. I asked my grandmother, who was sitting in the chair beside me reading her bible, to hold my hand. She replied, "I wasn't holding your hand when you were making that baby." She didn't know the real story. I never told anyone, and you are learning about this part of my life with the rest of the world and my family members. I could have swallowed myself because it took me back to the time and space when that incident took place. I couldn't dwell on that long because my son was ready to make his world debut. The nurse told me not to push because the doctor was on the way. It was too late because he was on the table. The doctor entered the room just in time to cut the umbilical cord. On March 7, 1991, not only was my son born, but I was reborn as the woman I am today. Everyday life was different from that day forth. I had a child who was solely dependent on the decisions I made.

I applied to Fort Valley State University with the same original goal: TO BECOME A DOCTOR, BY ANY MEANS NECESSARY. I arrived on campus, realizing I had been given another chance to either make the best of this opportunity or squander it. A college professor quickly told me, "You can either pay now and play later, or you can play now and pay later." That phrase resonated with me for the rest of my life. It stuck with me so much that I found myself inundated in my major. I spent long nights in the science building, so I could get ahead by studying the slides and models. Subliminally, I think that I was alienating myself from others, so I could stay out of harm's way. After commuting for two years, my grand-mother decided to allow me to finish my last year on campus. She took care of my child because she saw I was determined to make it. I had a prayer warrior in my corner. Everybody deserves a pray-ing grandmother.

I began to acclimate myself to campus life and developed lifelong friendships. My work ethic was evident then. My roommate and friends thought I was insane, but I had a goal and was laser focused on accomplishing it. For me, becom-ing a doctor would empower me with the skill set and the opportunity to write my own ticket in life. I would not only be able to take care of myself but also the wonderful gift God had given me, my son. The decision to keep him was the best one I have made to date. I became grounded and more committed to taking my education seriously, so it could lead to opportunities. I told myself to never give up. Even through the struggles, I learned things about myself. They groomed me for the stamina and courage I would need in the future. It would happen all in God's time.

Fast forward to the end of my junior year in college. During this year, I was introduced to the chiropractic field as a viable career and not just a service that I received with my grandmother (Yes, black people go to the chiropractor, and we had one growing up.) A recruiter from Life University came to our school and offered me an opportunity (for free) to visit the campus and stay in Atlanta for two weeks. I had nothing to lose. I had already made up my mind to attend the Medical College of Georgia in Augusta. This was a free, all-expense paid trip. Who knew this two-week program would change the trajectory of my life? I was sold, and my paradigm shift was immediate. I eagerly put in my application for chiropractic school. I was accepted on provisional admission, with the expectation of me graduating and passing the entrance criteria. My senior year in college was filled with all the possibilities and hopes for myself, my family, and my legacy.

Graduation day was finally here, and it was bittersweet. My grandmother was proud to have a generation of college graduates in her legacy, but

I was again leaving my safe place to forge ahead to the unknown. I was now in a bigger city with far more people than in my small hometown. It was very difficult to relate at times because I grew up differently than most of my cohorts. I quickly learned to get out of my comfort zone, make new friends, learn new cultures, and learn new ways of life. And for me, that's just part of growing up. I then took the steps to do what I needed to do to navigate my newfound world. The space I was traveling in was very intimidating. There were not a lot of women, and there were certainly not a lot of Black people in chiropractic at the time. The campus was situated in the heart of Marietta, which came with its own controversy for a Black, American female. On campus, I was treated okay, but off campus, it was another story. Cobb County was riddled with a lot of prejudices towards Black people, and then to be getting an education on top of this came with a lot a harassment. One of the many incidents I experienced was another student running me over with their car (physical body), and then accusing me of causing the damages to their car stating that I shouldn't have been standing in the parking space. To make matters worse, her boyfriend's brother, who was a police officer in Cobb County, arrested me for "hit and run" and used an existing scratch on my car as the catalyst to "put me in the system." This was a very difficult pill to swallow. I was not expecting to be a victim of prejudice while in chiropractic school. I did everything right (so I thought) to keep my nose clean, and still, outside forces were threatening my opportunity. I had to pay restitution for something I didn't do. The bigger picture for me was my goal: TO BECOME A DOCTOR. So, I did what needed to be done to move forward. Did it feel good? No, but I did it.

My second year of chiropractic school was my son's first year of school. I remember telling him each day before we both went off to school to get his backpack and Mommy has to get hers. There was always a struggle trying to keep up the delicate balance of being a full-time mom, full-time student, and working a full-time job. If it were not for the support system I had, I just don't know. My extended family were friends of my sister and church family I met. My new family served as a basis for needed services like babysitters, snack providers, surrogate aunties, and sounding boards to keep me focused. (Did I mention that I had ADD on top of all of this?) After finally getting into the flow of my new environment, I decided to move closer to my support system. Moving was a great decision for me and my family. I remember moving day like it was yesterday because it was both stressful and rewarding. On this day, I received some news from Cobb County. I was sent a letter stating that the officer who filed the case against me was found guilty and was discharged for using his authority inappropriately. My case was one of the ones in question, and my record was cleared. Hooray! I later found out that he was killed by some really bad people, and as they say, KARMA IS A $%#&^.

Four years pass by quickly when you are focused on one goal: TO BECOME A DOCTOR. It's graduation day. Here we are now at graduation number two, and I am now a fully credentialed and certified chiropractor who was ready to take on the universe. My grandmother was so happy that day. You would have thought that it was her graduation, and quite frankly, it was. She afforded me an opportunity many are not given, and that was for me to finish school. I presented her with a PHT (putting her through) degree. You would have thought that I had given her a million dollars. She was that proud.

CHAPTER 2

EARLY PRACTICE = LIFE LESSONS

I left graduation full of expectation and a willing-ness to do whatever it took to succeed. I was not going to let a few mishaps keep me from the life I knew I could have for me and my son. I went out into the world to acquire a job. I never went into this with a mindset of working for someone; however, I always understood if you don't have the tools to do something, you have to get help. When obtaining this master plan to success, you must be willing to do one of two things. You either pay someone to teach you the skills or you learn while you earn. I chose to do both. So, I embarked on getting involved in my community. I created an organizational chart on which individuals I was going to connect with and which institutions I was going to partner with to achieve my goal. I was eager, energetic, and excited about building my base to launch my practice. The first thing I learned was rejection is real, and it doesn't feel good. I had to learn how to interact in spite of the rejection that was happening to me. I had to adopt a mentality that I wasn't being rejected, but the time may have not been the best to implement my greatness. This mental skill did not develop overnight nor did it stem from positive energy, like the kind I am feeling at this moment. I was getting rejection after rejection for associate positions. I called every chiropractor in Macon and Middle Georgia, and they all said no. I was at the last name on my list. I worked my list in alphabetical order but skipped one name because I could not pronounce it. I mustered enough courage to make the phone call and was asked to come over for an interview. I was excited. I was finally getting my shot to make a mark on the world.

I arrived at the interview bright eyed and ready for what the day would bring. I looked up a few facts about the chiropractor and was amazed and intrigued with his background. He played professional baseball. I entered the practice and was escorted to the doctor's private office. The doctor immediately said, "I have never had an intern nor an associate, and quite frankly, I do not want one now." I can feel that day like it was today. I proceeded to gather my things together to leave. As I was getting up, the doctor said, "Something says to give you a chance." I thanked him for the opportunity, accepted his offer, and ran to the car, lifted my hands, and said thank you God for all you've done for me. What if I had given up after all the rejections?

After one year in this position, I started my private practice. I learned a tremendous amount of life skills and chiropractic approaches from this doctor. I worked three times as hard as most because I valued the education I had received from that experience, whether it was direct or indirect. He truly mentored me during that season. I learned what not to do as well as what to do on the other doctor's dime and time. Now, it was time to execute all the knowledge I had acquired. I used the little savings I had accumulated from waiting tables, the $4000 gift that my cousin, Al, gave me, and I quickly learned to leverage the good credit I had established as my seed money to start my first practice.

The first few years of practice were great. I had steadily built a clientele that valued my expertise and was willing to try something different. I was getting full remittance from the insurance companies. Little did I know that I had started during a time when the insurance companies were still paying 100 percent of the HCFA form, the form we use to send our procedure codes into the insurance company for them to consider, and that trend was coming to a screeching halt. I had all my credentials and all the bells and whistles. I started with a team of one and quickly had a team of three by the end of my third year. During my fifth year of practice, life was good. I was collecting at 80 percent, and monthly profits were ranging from $40,000 to $50,000 a month. I had mastered systems that were generating a profitable business and had a team of six employees, but my private life was in turmoil.

I was dating a guy who I thought was sincere, honest, and kind. My family didn't like him because they had heard some rumors. Of course, thinking I was in love kept me blind as information was surfacing. I later found out that he was embezzling funds from my accounts to bank roll his lifestyle and now family. I was devastated. I remember that hot, sweltering day in the summer of 2006 when I was forced to file bankruptcy and liquidate all my assets to repay outstanding bills he had accumulated. This accumulation was due to the blatant disregard to handling my affairs. I can still smell the trash from the alley as I was packing up the remainder of my things that were left behind. I cried the entire time thinking that if I ever recovered from this situation, it would never ever happen again. I was down, but I wasn't out.

I decided to take two years off to regroup and reflect on what took place in my practice. I went to Atlanta to work in another chiropractor's office. While in Atlanta, I used the time to get back to my theatrical roots and did both local and regional theater. I spent my spare time reassessing what systems worked in my business model and the things that I would do differently when I reopened my practice. I also shadowed a few doctors offering my services for free to learn and observe. I learned that there was nothing wrong with the "systems;" however, there was something wrong with MY system. I was attracting men who were emotional, financial, and spiritual vacuums. This was the time for self-care and the much-needed soul work that propelled me to be at the top of my industry. I, first, had to eliminate all the self-doubt, guilt, shame, and the embarrassment I was carrying around with me from all the negative encounters I had along the way. The emotional backpacks were keeping me from my one, true purpose and that was to empower others.

I just was unaware that I needed these experiences to do so. I took this time to work with both a clinical and a spiritual therapist. Through the course of many sessions, I was able to let go and exercise in my full capacity. During the time that I was going to a psychiatrist, it was taboo to talk about going to one let alone going to one as a member of the Black community. I had to travel that road alone, but I made it through. God planted a dream that had grown into my purpose. Now, it was time to get out of labor and give birth.

I had a good friend say to me that they were "damaged goods." I remember feeling like this prior to "doing the work." What I mean by doing the work is time spent with the therapist to implement my new mindset. Now, my reply is there is no such thing as damaged goods just redirected goods. We can either redirect ourselves in a positive or negative direction. I chose to redirect positively. It is crazy how people get mad at you for overcoming your issues. Instead of praising your triumphs, they choose to hurt you because they are not ready to do their own soul work. Go figure.

I moved back home with a plan of action. After conquering my self-doubt and embracing my self-worth, I decided to go back to school to get

my master's in International Business Adminis-
tration. I realized I didn't get the foundation from
chiropractic school I needed to fully understand
the business operations I had been outsourcing
to others. I vowed to never have a business where
I didn't know how to do every single thing that
came with running it. My question to myself was
how would I know if anything was done wrong if
I didn't know what "right" looked like. I received
my MBA and was now equipped with the business
acumen to add to the experience I had acquired.
I also was in a better situation to negotiate con-
tracts and navigate the business world on my
own. This cut my expenses in half.

By this time, my son was graduating from
high school. I was focused on making sure he was
secure in getting his education. He was admitted
to Fort Valley State University, my alma mater. I
was so proud. On a visit to the college, I ran into
an old college professor of mine. She asked me if I
would be interested in an opportunity to teach at
the university. I jumped on the chance to lecture
at my dear Fort Valley State University. I saw this
as an opportunity to give back to the university
that had instilled so many lessons in me.

I began teaching undergraduate classes in the science department. I was teaching biology for non-majors and anatomy and physiology for majors. I confidently strolled into all my classes with the hopes of imparting the science knowledge and the life lessons that were given to me. I was stern but fair. Many of the students I taught were future doctors and healthcare providers. I wanted them to understand how competitive the field was, as well as understand the need for more people of color to serve. I also taught the students to understand deadlines, commitments, and critical thinking. I had a no-nonsense demeanor, and the students and my colleagues knew I was about business. I was tough on my students because I wanted to see them succeed. I gave them the same "pay now" speech that was given to me, and I made future doctors. I still get thank you cards, letters, gifts, and invitations from previous students thanking me for getting them ready for the big leagues. I created a legacy.

While at the university, I learned that the school would no longer sell sorority and fraternity paraphernalia. I saw this challenge as an opportunity to diversify my portfolio. You must always be ready to move when an opportunity presents itself. You should be in "drive" position when your big break comes. So, that's what I did. I researched what was needed and opened a paraphernalia store in 2009. Who knew the money I accumulated from this business would give me what I needed to relaunch my practice? Things truly happen for a reason.

While continuing to teach at Fort Valley State, I decided to start networking with attorneys, medical doctors, and rehabilitation facilities. I wanted them to know I was re-branding my practice and wanted them to support me as they had done in the past. BAD MISTAKE. I put myself out there too quickly because the patients started rolling in, and the facility where I currently practice was still being built out. I was placed in a conundrum. What to do? I called all the chiropractors in town and asked them if I could rent a space to see patients until my office was ready. No one was interested in managing an independent contractor. Remember, these are the same doctors who didn't give me a chance to work in their practices. I called one last doctor who agreed to let me do work in their office. I was so excited I forgot to do the most important thing, call my attorney to draft a contract. This was another valuable lesson I learned. It would come back to haunt me later. The doctor and I had a conversation concluding my rent payment would be 40 percent of my collections. I would have full use of the premises, equipment, and staff. I had the number one attorney in town referring me patients. I was swamped and making a lot of money for the other doctor. Yes, you read it right, the other doctor. I didn't get one penny from any of those cases. The attorney was forwarding the checks to the business entity and not me. The fees from the patients I was seeing who were paying cash or submitting payments from insurance claims were not paid to me either because the billing department was told by the other doctor to file them under his name. THIS IS FRAUD. I asked for a meeting with the doctor about my money, and I even recorded the conversation. I used the tape to stop future payments, so they went to me directly and transferred all my patients to my new office. Needless to say, the other doctor's mishandling of my collections caused the doctor to not only lose the trust of the attorney, but he also lost patients and ultimately within four years, his business. A bulk of those patients are now currently being treated in my practice. They didn't trust him. His business lacked INTEGRITY.

I started revamping my business. I used the systems that worked and restructured those that didn't. I was now in a better place mentally for success. I am sharing my deepest darkest secrets with you, so you can overcome the first step in being successful in business, and that's owning who you are and unapologetically loving who you are as well as embracing the journey that got you to where you are today. Nothing that has happened in your past can stop you from creating a better future. Only you can determine what the future holds for you. I had patients who I had previously treated who were overly excited to come back to the culture I had in my office. I also got business from many women who wanted to be seen by a female chiropractor because they felt comfortable in that environment. Through proper networking, I got the support of the medical community as a resource for chronic neck and low back pain and was placed on most of the worker's compensation plans. I was on a mission, and this time I was not going to get distracted. I was on target meeting the goals I had set. My customers were my top priority. Over the years,

I have learned that it does not matter what you sell, but it matters what kind of an experience your patient wants. I can say with full affirmation I win because of faith, courage, and execution. All the things that appeared as failures were only maps for the success I have today. It has created a compilation of resources and connections for me to help others on their journeys as well.

CHAPTER 3

WHY SOME DON'T MAKE IT IN BUSINESS

The common reason why new businesses close is because they don't have enough money. Starting a business like mine can cost anywhere from $45,000 to $90,000 or more. Cash flow is crucial to any business startup. You must budget and penny pinch by only buying what you need. Avoid making large cash purchases and use other financing options like leasing, so you can have your cash on hand and in your bank account. You need to keep your doors open long enough to create a steady flow of paying clients.

When you start your business, don't buy too much. Too much overhead can kill a business just as fast as not having enough money. Starting out, I know you want the best; however, we must crawl before we walk. You should focus on surviving your first year. There are three questions I asked myself when I started out:

1. How much space (square footage) do I need?
2. How many tables/equipment (insert your tools of your trade) do I need?
3. How much can I spend on Electronic Health Records (the systems and trade software that allow me to do my job proficiently)?

When you are budgeting for your office, you should budget with the bare necessities in mind and get other equipment as those needs arise. When looking for a space, try to find an option that is already built to suit as possible. This keeps you from spending unnecessary money (that you don't have) for build out. Remember, you have not made any money, and you are not truly profitable until all your expenses are paid, and you are paying your monthly expenses as well. I would even take it a step further and say make sure you have six months of monthly expenses saved up on reserve both personally and businesswise.

When I was teaching college, I told students to stop overwhelming themselves with every single detail when planning something. Psychologist, Barry Schwartz, coined the phrase "Paradox of Choice" to describe his consistent findings emphasizing, "while increased choice allows us to achieve objectively better results, it also leads to greater anxiety, indecision, paralysis, and dissatisfaction." Many business scholars also understand the term paralysis by analysis. Stop overthinking and planning too much. We are not psychic and cannot foresee all the possible things that could happen when we start a business. Don't worry. Start planning with these three questions:

1. Are you compliant with all the regulations of the federal, state, and local governments?
2. Are you required to carry a license in your state for your trade?
3. Do you have the minimum of what you need to open (table, computer, EHR, etc.)?

Set a date and OPEN!
It is better to get started and not be perfect than to never start at all. This is called imperfect execution.

There has been many articles and books written on this subject if you want to learn more.

Okay, so on the other side of this coin is too little planning or not planning enough. You will struggle in business if you fail to plan. You must have a business plan. Start your business plan first and follow it. Remember, it is a dynamic document, which means it is always changing. You also need to have a system in place on how you are going to get clients in your doors once you are open. You need to know what your business structure will be as well as your standard operating procedures. I heard someone say one of the reasons most business startups fail is due to lack of execution. I agree. It is the fuel of your business plan. You can dream it, put it on paper, but if you don't do anything, it still doesn't matter. It takes a lot of perspiration to win at anything. Strategic execution brings rivers of revenue, but mere dreaming yields excuses and emptiness. You must put in the hours, days, months, and years to be successful. Any great athlete must put in an enormous amount of time and training to be at the top of their game. As a leader in business, I had to go through many years of tests, trials, mishaps, and disappointments in order to help others succeed. This is how my systems were birthed. My mother would say, "You don't have to bump your head on the brick wall to know that it will hurt." So, why make the same mistakes I made if you don't have to? Benefit from my voyage and learn from my mistakes, so you don't spend unnecessary capital or worse, never start.

Take responsibility for yourself and your actions. Take hold of your life. Excuses are not accepted. This is a personal journey, and you must go get it. Habits really do make or break you. Good habits in business will lead to credibility, reliability, and personal connections in your industry. Daily routines and procedures will show you what is important to you. It will bring to light your priorities. If you spend all your day on social media, then that is your priority. If you spend all day on gossiping, then that's a priority. Bad habits will get you off track. Without proper habits, you will produce fruit from the seeds of poor planning. But if you spend your time meditating on the success of your practice and honing up on your skills, then that's a priority. Good habits keep you on track. Proper habits will produce fruit from your seeds of properly planning.

Credibility is what you know well. It is what makes you the leader and authority on your subject matter. An assumption is made that you know what you are doing when you have the credentials to do your craft, i.e., education, licenses, and certifications. However, it doesn't stop there. You should always be studying your craft. Are you searching daily for articles, books, and journals with the latest information on what you are doing? If the answer is yes, you are creating credibility with your customer base. If the answer is no, shift your actions now, so you can exercise credible habits. Credibility is the respect your business has, and it displays honesty. When you are honest, you are living with integrity. This allows you to live in your truth. Only you know what that looks like. Do what is right, and you will never have to think about anybody looking at what you are doing trying to find ways to get you into trouble.

Reliability is being there and doing what you say all the time. Can your patients, clients, or customers count on you? Think about this for a moment. You have a place you love to buy clothing from. They are one of three stores that sells your favorite brand. You know their hours of operations and exactly where to find your go-to outfit when you go inside. You have been going to this establishment for five years. It's Saturday, and when you get to the door, there's a sign stating, "Be back in 15 minutes." So, you brush it off, and you come back on a different day, and low and behold, the sign is still posted. Will you continue doing business with this company? I tend to think not. That business is no longer reliable. Remember, there are two other businesses in town that are eager to separate you from your money. It is important to sustain the same results over and over again. Dependable outcomes lead to long-term customer compliance. So, make sure you open every day at the same time and make sure there is always a qualified, knowledgeable representative to take care of your most important asset, your ideal client. Make sure the service and/or product is STELLAR. Make sure your client can bet the bank they will receive consistency from you. This is accomplished by placing a system of methods that keep your mission, values, and goals in the forefront.

Personal connection is the level of engagement you have with your client base. Are you taking the time to connect with others that makes them want to do business with you? Are you giving people extraordinary services and interactions that compels them to share with others? This type of connection creates a sense of belonging and engagement with you and/or your product. This is truly an organic, grassroots moment for you to attract others to what you have to offer. This, in turn, creates repeat clientele who will advertise for you. It forms a ripple effect with returning and new patients, clients, and customers. In my practice, when patients walk into the office, everyone upfront stands immediately and welcomes them into our office with a warm friendly smile. A beverage is offered, and we show them where the restroom is located. We have them take a seat for further directions. I compare the experience to someone visiting my home. I wouldn't leave my door open for anyone to walk in without standing at or near the door to welcome them in. I would also show hospitality by offering something to drink and offering the use of the restroom. This simple gesture is why we have patients screaming from the rooftops to their friends and families, so they can become a part of our healthcare family. The atmosphere is very serene and spa-like. People get to escape and relax when they are there. They truly feel safe. These are just a few examples of how we begin each visit with our patients. They know they are not just another diagnosis but a real friend to the business.

Not getting involved in your community through networking is causing you to miss out on vital connections. Now, don't get me wrong, social media and a great website are a good start, but you need real people to generate trust and word of mouth credibility about your skills in your community. Face-to-face connections plant the seeds to referrals. This can be anything from attending your child's PTA meeting to going to the function your local chamber of commerce hosts. When making connections, lead conversations learning about your new connection first. Never build relationships leading with your wants and needs. The way people feel around you will either make or break the trust. It has been proven repeatedly.

Risk is the probability of you performing with excellence. It is anything that could keep you from achieving your mission, values, and goals. Will you execute your mission and goals with a spirit of excellence? How are you showing up each day to solidify your place in the market? In other words, are your actions coinciding with the brand you are putting out in the world. This is a critical area that reduces overall trust in the community in which you are serving. There are certainly factors beyond your control that could create risk such as a decline in the market causing a recession. However, maintaining a healthy risk margin is the map that helps us find our way to SUCCESS. In my practice, I have established standard operating procedures, so there is congruency with how it is represented. I revamp these quarterly, and I also seek team members' input and reward them when they prevent apparent disasters.

Trust is the accumulation of credibility, reliability, and personal connection while factoring in the risk that you may or may not live up to the demands, pressures, and outlooks in your business. It is the most important asset your brand has. People want to do business with people who they value and trust. You want to make sure your credibility, reliability, and personal connections are of the highest value, and your risk is low. We are not perfect, and there is no such thing as a perfect business model. However, we can strive to operate our business where we strive to get to 100 percent each day. In my practice, transparency is the key to trust. In our process, we take each patient through financial counseling, so they are aware of what their financial responsibilities will be before I ever enter the room. I think it's irresponsible to assume that the average consumer understands their insurance policy. The major confusion we have to tackle is teaching the difference between what a deductible (the amount you are responsible for before the insurance starts to pay) and an out of pocket cost is (the amount you can accumulate through the deductible and co-pays, so the insurance can start to pay at 100 percent).

CHAPTER 4

FACE YOUR FEAR

Fear is something that is made in the mind. It simply is not real. If you put the energy of worry and fear in the atmosphere, the atmosphere will give that same worry and fear back to you. My acronym for fear is False Energy Affecting Reality. Are you projecting things that are misleading to yourself and others? Are you filling your spirit with deceit? Are your thoughts keeping you from moving in a positive direction? Is your existence warped? If so, the moment you truly understand the meaning of fear you can start to do something about it. Say it with me three times: IT IS FAKE, IT IS A SCAM, IT IS A HOAX.

So, the real question is why are people naturally afraid? The adage says we fear the unknown. That's very true, but how do you confront that? The answer is so simple that it's embarrassing. It is summed up into two words; CONQUER IT!!!! Sometimes this is easier said than done. This is a process on its own that could take several months or even years to do. You must face fear head on, or it will keep you from obtaining your purpose. How is this done? Through my interactive approach.

Step 1:
You must write your fear(s) down
on an index card.

Step 2:
For 45 days, you will tell that fear that
it does not exist.
Say it with me three times:
IT IS FAKE,
IT IS A SCAM,
IT IS A HOAX.

Step 3:
For 45 days, write down or do a social media post
saying words of affirmation for your life.

So, a great example in your business would be applying for a business loan. The thought of going to a bank and asking them to finance your dream seems daunting for most to say the least. Acknowledging that the fear is a deception in your mind and telling the heavens it doesn't exist creates a ripple effect for faith to take over. By going through the loan process, you are conditioning your brain to exhibit healthy thought processes concerning the very incident you were afraid of. Actively engaging in the process helps you become more comfortable with it, and thus, you are no longer afraid of the unknown. There is something known as paralysis in the medical world. It causes your muscles to no longer function as they once did. This concept is totally true when it comes to business. We can become mentally paralyzed. This happens when we get overwhelmed and start to procrastinate. This happens more often with doctors and high functioning executives. You become so distracted with the process of being perfect you fail to start or launch any idea. You then start doing other things, so you don't have to deal with the task at hand. This stops the revenue train dead in its tracks. I fondly call this "lack of action." Instead of just starting the task without being perfect, you sabotage the whole project due to doing nothing.

CHAPTER 5

FOCUS ON WHAT MATTERS

What are the things that matter most to you? Is it family, friends, or fulfillment? The thing that is most important to me is my faith. No matter what your spiritual background is, we should always believe in a power that is greater than ourselves. Faith yields gratitude. You should be grateful in all things concerning you and your business. You must show gratitude for what you have at every step of the journey. The more you exercise gratitude, the better you feel. When you feel better, you do better, and when you do better, you become success minded. I choose to call my higher power God. God has innately given you a purpose. Follow that purpose. If you operate in your purpose, the money will follow your purpose instead of you running after the money. You must take the time to meditate or pray to God. Nothing is more important than plugging into the source and experiencing the fullness of God in your life. When you do those things that honor your faith, the God that lives in you comes alive. So, what is your purpose? Your purpose is the thing you can do without hesitation. Simply stay in your lane and maximize it. I was taught to be a doctor, but I was born to inspire and empower. I am a conservationist. I like to tell stories and help others through sharing my experiences. In other words, I like to talk to people. My pastor says, "Your job is what you are paid to do, but your purpose is what you are made to do." The beautiful thing is they can be one and the same. You do not know what your purpose is because you haven't asked God nor do you seek him first in all things.

After God, my family is the cornerstone to my vitality. Scientifically, relationships are required for a long life. We need the love and nurturing of family to feel secure and needed. Sometimes when we are yearning after the things the world says are important, we forget about the very people who are vital to our longevity. It is important to find the exact balance between ambition and family life. This is vital to success. It would be in vain to put all the effort in amassing all your wealth, and your family never reaps the benefits of a healthy relationship with you. Experiences and memories are essential to quality of life. This is one of the areas that adds life to your years. As a small child, I never knew we were poor because of the love my grandmother gave. She nurtured us with patience, goodness, hope, and trust. Family dynamics can either support or retard your success. A supportive family can provide stability, capital, or even a helping hand when you start your business. That support may come in a form you may never have expected. For an example, I didn't include my cousin, Al, in the equation when I wrote my business plan. However, when I asked, he provided the seed money needed. Channel positive energy as fuel to keep you focused. Remember, everyone will not be happy for you. The haters are real. Haters can come in many forms even family and friends. When you stay focused on your vision, your perspective on things can change. Situations that would have caused you to give up no longer matter.

The next thing that matters to me is service to others. I love serving others. All the career paths I have had have been in customer service. I believe in serving my community with a willing heart. I want to do it; I don't have to do it. Having the character to give will put you in positions of high places. It happened in my life. I get to take care of the very fabric of what makes my community rich and sound, PEOPLE. Through this commitment, I was elected as a commissioner to sit on the Water Authority Board. Now, that's favor.

Be humble and exercise patience. Patience is power. Don't quit. Remember, the adage says quitters never win, and winners never quit. Nothing worthwhile comes easy. It takes work and a lot of it. It takes planning to become successful. You must create a strategy to reach your goals. Give it your all. Give whatever you do 150 percent of your efforts, time, and space. The end result will be worth the sacrifice even if you get off track. It is never too late to get back on track. You are not in a race. You are always in competition to better yourself. No one will believe in you until you do. Back yourself. You can do this.

CHAPTER 6

LEAN INTO CHALLENGES

When you are doing something you love, you make time for it. This is essential for any business. You must be present. Also, loving others is a characteristic of successful business owners. People will work hard for you when they know you care about them and their needs. A challenge in today's business world is that most are only focused on the bottom line. Biggy Smalls said, "It's all about the Benjamin's baby." However, in order for your company to experience significant revenues, you need help. We are in the people business. We need people to purchase our services and/or products. Because we are human and have emotions, this can present an issue if you don't have your game face and attitude set for customer service. No matter how you feel, you must always put yourself in your client's shoes. Everyone deserves to be honored and respected no matter how much money they have. But this is your business, and people are paying you for your expertise and are expecting it without any constraints. The fact that I am a healthcare provider in the wellness industry keeps me focused on encouraging an environment of tranquility.

Setting proper goals are important. Without direction, you will end up executing the wrong goals. Goals allow you to know where you are going. This keeps you focused, so you don't end up doing things that are not relevant to the goal. You need to know, so if someone or something tries to take you off course, you can say "NO." Saying no to others means saying yes to your vision, your mission, and your goals. You have things to do, and time is of the essence. Time management skills help, and a willingness to accomplish the things with a deadline keeps your business feasible.

Change your focus. Keep your eyes on what you expect and not on the journey itself. You must endure and push through the pain, adversities, and the difficult times. You need to have a clear vision of what you want to do, so you are not distracted from the end result you desire Your life depends on it.

CHAPTER 7

TAKE RISKS

In order to succeed in business, you must take risks. The biggest risk to your business is not taking a risk. Life is a series of calculated risk. Everything we do in life has some level of risk. Nothing is foolproof. When we get in our car and drive each day, we are taking a risk that we may get in a car accident. There is a chance we won't even make it to our destination. The life you want and the business you want to grow depends on the choices you make daily. Now, I am not suggesting that you do something risky like being left in the Serengeti with all the wildlife of Africa without a proper guide.

Do you know how risky it was for me to start my first business? I was the second woman and the first Black person to open a chiropractic practice in my area. I had no mentor to help guide me through the process. I had to execute quickly. At the time, I didn't have any business acumen. What I did have was faith, and I knew how to serve others. I knew to hire others when I could not do something. I had properly planned as much as I could to reduce my risk exposure. I, now, understand the pitfalls and can help you, so you have a solution in place.

Risk taking deeply encourages accountability. As a business owner, you are responsible for everything-for better or for worse. If you truly believe your new service or product will move the company towards profitability, then it's a risk worth taking. If the idea works, you make money. However, if it doesn't work, just take ownership of it and don't play the blame game. Accountability also can minimize risk. Only through clearly understanding, identifying, and managing risk as a responsibility of the entire team will you create a culture of accountability in your business. A framework should be in place to ensure that the team understands who's responsible and what those potential risks are. A great example in my office is the handling of patients' information. I make sure there is a privacy practice class all employees must attend in order to understand the process. It is important that everyone knows the risks that are involved in collecting our patients' information. We also go over the consequences that could occur if things are not compliant.

Trust the process. I know you probably have seen this term a million times in your reading, but it is steadfast, tried, and true. The process never changes; people do. This is called a calculated risk. You know the outcome when you do the steps. This is a long-term plan, and it sometimes is not comfortable. Do not doubt yourself and never take short cuts. If you show up, use your skill set, and work your mindset; you will yield RESULTS. When you stop doing these things, the outcome will be detrimental.

Evaluate your business risks regularly. You should perform this assessment each quarter. In evaluating your risks, you determine whether it is in the best interest of the business to take action to prevent or minimize exposure. You must prioritize risks by ranking them once you have identified them. For example, in my practice, anyone who is responsible for any data, server's network, or software, must perform a risk evaluation. We want to make sure our patients' information is not at risk from hackers or lost due to a natural disaster.

Revamping your business model is another way to assess risk. Remember, the competition is always looking to one up every competitor.

So, it is important that you assess your risk, so your competitors don't gain an advantage that can prevent you from reaching the goals you have set for your enterprise. Are they providing a cheaper cost with a better product? Are they in a better location? Do they have better benefits for your human resources? Has your competition launched a new product using technology of the future? Those are definitely questions you should be considering in your business.

CHAPTER 8

FIND LESSONS IN FAILURE

Be willing to FAIL: Find Another Initiative and Learn or Find Another Idea to Launch. So, what if it doesn't work out? Are you going to give up? If it's your purpose, then you don't have a choice but to keep moving forward. There is no such thing as failure. This process is just as important as the success side of the spectrum because you become wiser if you learn from it. You truly become an expert. So, I find another way to do it, and maybe this time, it will work. If not, learn and try again. Maybe that wasn't the best idea you came up with. Get over it and think of a new one. Fail quickly.

Handling failure starts with a strong, positive attitude. It takes a "stick with it" attitude to keep at it after things don't work out. This is where most business owners struggle. You must learn how to handle failure by accepting it along with the rejection and move on to the task that makes you money. I have a natural sense of humor, so I find failure as an opportunity to further develop my sense of humor. I find myself telling people all the time about some of the mistakes I made, and the same thing I cried all night long about is suddenly hilarious. I have made a commitment to myself to laugh sooner and do a happy dance.

Learn from your failure. No matter how many times I had to start over and regroup, I learned something. Every successful person I studied "failed" according to world standards but learned what to do as well as what not to do as a result of it. Failure creates tons of learning experiences. It gives me another chance to hone my skills of persuasion. The more people I meet, the more money I make. The one that takes the highest risk gets the biggest spoils. There are many things that can affect your business, but they are all temporary if you have a good attitude.

CHAPTER 9

TAKE ACTION TODAY

I love Nike's campaign slogan, "JUST DO IT." That speaks volumes. This effortless message says to the world to get out and execute. You must take responsibility for putting something in motion without regret or inner judgment. By taking action, you are telling the world "I am good enough, I am strong enough, and I am willing to take whatever life gives me." You are also honoring God by being flexible to reach your purpose. Stop slapping God in the face when you don't use your gifts. Stand in your greatness. What do you have to lose? Better yet, think on all the things you must gain. Doing nothing will provide the same result, NOTHING. So, it's absolutely important to not get ready to take action, but you must TAKE ACTION. By taking action, you create a sense of urgency which is a driver for success. This is how you take your power to succeed back. Here are three steps to take action:

1. Change your story. Where do you want to go? What are your goals?
2. Seek out opportunities. What do you know, and what are you good at doing?
3. Keep taking action. What do you need to learn in order to act? What are the threats that are standing in your way?

Being perfect is a delusion. There's no such thing as a perfect human being. Follow your own path. Stop trying to do things like others. Your service and/or product is unique because of YOU. There's a proclamation I say daily in the mirror. Repeat after me: I am the best, I do the best, I expect the best, I receive the best because I AM UNIQUELY ME. Now, I want you to write this on at least five index cards. Place one on each mirror of your home, car, and desk area at work. Remember, you are the "special sauce," you are what makes your business special. No one can beat you at being you. Now, go THRIVE.

CHAPTER 10

RESTART QUICKLY

Are you ready for the restart? Do you have what it takes to be an entrepreneur? This is the first step in determining whether you should restart? The "entrepreneurial spirit" is something you either have or you don't. There have been many who have tried to open a business and got out quickly because they just didn't have the intestinal fortitude and the mindset that is necessary to thrive in this capacity. An entrepreneur thinks differently from an employee. Entrepreneurs are people who are resourceful, take action, take risks, welcome change, never afraid of hard work, futuristic, obsesses over cash flow, and doesn't ask permission. They also seek challenges as opportunities, challenge the status quo, are very disciplined, and passionate. I knew from a young age I wanted to work for myself. My grandmother challenging me at a young age to turn fifty dollars into the much-needed funds to go on a band trip fueled my inner businesswoman. It was a feeling I just can't explain. It was an inner drive to set goals and achieve them. The initial goal was to just flip the fifty dollars to three hundred and fifty dollars. However, we kept going and reinvesting in the business. It didn't make sense to me to be on a job for 30 years and have a company watch to display for your hard work. Now, don't get me wrong, there is honor in working hard. All good businesses need good people to work for them. It just didn't fit my mindset. For you to realize your dreams, you must create a series of small goals that lead up to a larger goal. This will motivate your success along the way. Have a daily schedule that works for you, so you can make the most of your time and abilities, and you will stick with it. Set aside some time to work on your business each day to stay driven to make things happen. This is just the tip of the iceberg as it relates to thinking differently. Your circle will change and get smaller as you pursue your business. But you can do it.

Reviving your business is the second step in starting over. A great way to do this is with branding. Sometimes, you need to freshen up your content, services, and products and relaunch with a more relatable logo that speaks to your consumer's behavior. It will describe your ideal client's mindset and attitudes, which in turn will help you make better decisions which leads to more MONEY. We don't have the luxury to be irresponsible with our brand. It must be protected. We must be wise in how it's executed.

Step three is to shine bright and smile always. This is the added value I brought to the table while quickly adapting to my new environment in chiropractic school. Those words helped me develop my mission, vision, core values, and goals for my business. My mission is to educate and empower business owners to start their own businesses, sharpen their business acumen, and turn their life goals into action. What is your purpose for your business? Developing a good mission will let your customer base know why you exist and what services will be provided. When developing my vision statement, I had to make sure it was clear and concise. My vision is simply that our company will be the leading provider of programs and services geared toward successfully starting a business without making costly mistakes. This sets the direction for my company. What does your company believe in or stand for? These are your core values which create the culture of your organization, and it must be what you are doing. Core values should describe the attributes of your business. My core values are to educate the world about chiropractic care and wellness, to empower the world to add life to their years through a holistic approach, to create raving fans with stellar service, to be the leader of quality care for personal injury and rehabilitation services, and to maintain a culture that is vitalistic in an environment that is tranquil. Lastly, the goals that you set help initiate a plan of action for your company. My goals include providing the highest quality product with personal customer service, competitive pricing, increasing revenue to over $3 million by year five while limiting expenses, increasing client base by 450 percent in five years, diversifying and growing revenue streams, maintaining job costing that keeps margins above 70 percent, and ensuring financial sustainability. Remember, goals can evolve as your business changes.

As a leader, you are entrusted with a lot of demanding responsibilities. But a successful leader not only deals with responsibilities but also thrives in the face of challenges. So, no matter the industry, those who know how to plan, anticipate, delegate, and appreciate, finish strong.

There are a lot of moving parts in the day to day operations of your business. Building a dynamic team both externally and internally is critical to your success. An external team would be getting a good attorney, accountant, financial planner, and a bookkeeper. The internal team would be a receptionist, billing/insurance specialist, medical billing/coder, and an assistant. Getting people to work together effectively can be challenging. When one person or department isn't doing their job, it can impact the entire company. It doesn't matter if it's two or three hundred people. In my career, 60 percent of your success is due to having the right people on your team. Do you have the desired people to get you to the right place? Are they the best fit for the culture of your business? I can guarantee you that every successful business owner has some type of company vision, mission, and goals in place. It is important for the overall culture of your business to share it with your employees. Clearly communicating your outcomes and expectations to your team will translate to consistency, respect, and transparency among your team. Everyone who represents the brand must buy into the culture and be able to extend the same level of commitment to compliance as you would. At some point, you must trust your team to do what you've trained them to do and release the control. The remaining 40 percent is strategy and operations. Strategy is your plan of action, so you know where you are going. Operations are your day to day procedures and how they are performed. The success of these are directly related to how your team executes your vision and expectations. Success comes from clear, effective leadership and employee support. Success is the goal, but it's the day to day interactions and operations that generate powerful results.

Never stop learning and working on yourself. Everyone has the potential to learn and grow. Every new learning opportunity gets us to the next level. You are never too old, young, or successful to learn. Read all the books, articles, and materials you can. Take classes, attend conferences, and do whatever it takes to understand what it means to be successful. Even at this stage of my career, I have a business coach who helps me to continue to get to the next level.

So, do you have what it takes to start over? Do you have the mental capacity to get the job done? Are you willing to put in the long hours and sacrifice time away from your friends and family? Are you willing to plant the seeds of success TODAY, so you can have the FREEDOM to explore the world? If your answer is YES, then it's time to get digging and do the real work.

[THANK YOU]

I would like to first thank God for making me in his image and for giving me a strong will to overcome everything that was meant to destroy me. I wrote this book to honor the legacy of my grandmother and to thank her for creating peace during the storms of my life. I want to thank my mother and father for telling me I could do anything. My mom is my biggest cheerleader, and I am grateful for that. I want to thank the love of my life, Deon Aiken, for being patient and tender. Thank you for enduring the long nights of me staying up to conceptualize this book. To my sister, Neidra, thank you for being my first best friend. I love you and the tribe. To my cousins, Al and Sondi, thank you for allowing God to use you to plant the seed into my first business. I will never forget that. Thank you to my business coach, Dr. Drai, for encouraging me to tell my story to the world. To all the people who will grow from this work, thank you. I want you to understand that through faith and perseverance, you can do anything. Remember the first step is to back yourself.

[ABOUT THE AUTHOR]

As one of the nation's most acclaimed business consultants and coaches, Dr. Anissa M. Jones (a.k.a. Dr. Nissa) is a board-certified chiropractor and the founder and clinical director of Total Fuze Chiropractic. In addition to providing a spa-like environment for her patients, she consistently works with other chiropractors and entrepreneurs to improve their business systems and increase their business acumen. As a nationally recognized author and speaker, Dr. Nissa also shares her business expertise via her YouTube series, Bossnomics.

Dr. Nissa earned her bachelor of science from Fort Valley State University, her international executive MBA from Wesleyan College, and her doctor of chiropractic from Life University. She is the first African American to practice chiropractic in Macon, Georgia. She is an enthusiastic volunteer with Alpha Kappa Alpha Sorority, Inc., and other charitable organizations in her hometown. Her spare time is spent traveling and singing.

Dr. Nissa has one son, Christian.

To learn more, visit drnissa.com

CREATING DISTINCTIVE BOOKS
WITH INTENTIONAL RESULTS

We're a collaborative group of creative masterminds
with a mission to produce high-quality books to position
you for monumental success in the marketplace.

Our professional team of writers, editors, designers,
and marketing strategists work closely together to ensure
that every detail of your book is a clear representation
of the message in your writing.

Want to know more?
Write to us at info@publishyourgift.com
or call (888) 949-6228

Discover great books, exclusive offers, and more at
www.PublishYourGift.com

Connect with us on social media

@publishyourgift